我只能好好吃

文／孟瑛如
圖／溫家豪、溫琬婷
英文翻譯／吳侑達

我只能好好吃，是的，我只能好好吃！

因為我，如如，自小就被確診為第一型糖尿病患者，必須學會與高血糖共存，就像醫生說的：「只能定時定量好好吃！」「飯吃七分飽，運動一定要，才能活到老！」

高糖、高鈉、高油脂或高膽固醇食物對我都是禁忌！

　　我不能跟大家一起搶營養午餐，我只能默默吃我定量的五穀飯及蔬菜魚肉。

　　同學們利用午休時間辦慶生會，帶來各種精緻糕點擺滿好幾張課桌椅，汽水、可樂、養樂多、果凍、布丁、糖果等任大家吃到飽，班上氣氛high到不行。然而，我只能在旁邊看著，拿出媽媽準備的水果盒，吃我的番石榴及番茄。

　　固定運動習慣對我很重要，但是體育課後我不能和同學一起喝珍珠奶茶或各種冰涼飲料，放學後也不能一起咬著熱狗、拿著爆漿紅豆餅、舔著霜淇淋或是吸著思樂冰走路回家。

　　有時我會很羨慕大家可以自由自在的吃任何食物，因為每當週一或是假期過後，同學們總會圍在一起高談闊論星期假日去哪裡吃了什麼好吃的好大雞排、吮指雞塊、×記豬腳、奶油酥餅等，我都只能一臉茫然，無法插嘴。

同學們還會在課餘組「美食團」，團購各種零食蛋糕或一起約出去吃美食，但他們很少約我。同學們找我一起去吃東西，最後結語總是：「妳很掃興耶！」或是「我看到妳吃東西的樣子就沒胃口了！」我也不知道該怎麼辦啊！

　　有些頑皮的同學會故意在我面前啃著炸雞腿或各種我不太能吃
的東西，還一面說：「好香呀！妳真是扛著口袋牽著馬，有福不
會享啊！」「不能吃×××，人生的樂趣就少掉三分之二了！」
我只好笑罵他們：「別引誘我啦！」「我如果亂吃東西，才真是
到了懸崖不勒馬，死路一條啊！」

　　有些不知情的同學還以為我是愛美保持身材，所以才吃得少、吃得巧。他們總是擔心的看著我，有時還會偷偷塞食物給我，怕我營養不夠。

這天老師上課時，我的人生轉機出現了！

老師上課的主題是：由如何吃才對？看歷年的「食安事件」。

「人活著每天都需要食物，要如何吃才能好好保健自己、愛惜自己？東西只能好好吃，不能隨便吃！」聽到這裡，我的精神都來了。「東西只能好好吃，不能隨便吃！」這不是跟我從小到大每次門診聽到醫師及營養衛教師說的話一樣嗎？

老師展示了用心製作的食安事件 PowerPoint 檔案：「食安問題：2011 年塑化劑汙染事件，濃縮果粉、果汁、果漿、優酪粉等五十多種飲料食品違法添加有毒塑化劑。」

「2014 年各種塑膠包裝食品含塑化劑事件。」台下的同學們一片驚呼：「天啊！這些我都常隨手灌一罐！」

　　老師說：「2013 年發生毒澱粉風暴，市售的粉圓、板條等產品，遭不當添加工業用黏著劑順丁烯二酸酐。」同學們聽了，眼珠瞪得更大了：「都是我愛吃的東西呢！」

老師接著說：「還有 2013 年的香精麵包事件。」有同學說：「那間店很有名呢！我媽還排隊去買！」

「製作麵包的膨鬆劑含鋁，麵包、吐司都中標。」老師又說。
同學直呼：「我每天早餐都吃麵包！有時還吃兩個，真噁！」

「2013 年還爆發食用油添加低成本葵花油及棉籽油混充，且添加銅葉綠素調色，這件事的影響層面非常廣。」老師繼續說明。「對啊！當時我們家裡還有兩桶，因為這品牌在大賣場常打折，我媽都買它！但後來我們都不敢再拿來用了。」一位同學說。

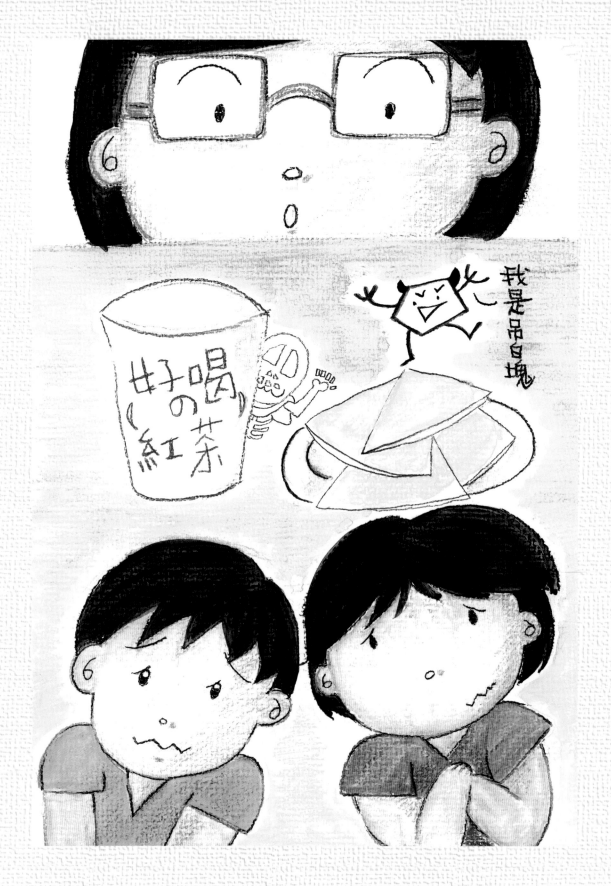

老師說：「有些潤餅皮添加了工業漂白劑吊白塊！」

有同學慘叫：「我最喜歡吃潤餅了！」

「手搖飲料店的茶類飲料也檢驗出殘留農藥！」這時同學們
都面色如土，因為班上有人每天至少一杯！

「說了這麼多，我們班有誰吃得最健康呢？」老師一問完，大家不約而同把臉轉向我，你一言我一語的說：「如如！班上她吃得最健康！」「如如最能抗拒垃圾食物的誘惑！」「如如從來不亂吃！」「如如都定時定量還運動！」

老師說：「對！我們班如如吃得最健康！只有如如不必擔心，因為她每餐都有好好吃。食物吃得對，時間吃得對，量控制得對，生活一定對！哈哈哈！」

「如如請站起來讓大家鼓掌一下！因為如如是全班飲食習慣最好的！」我開心的站起來接受大家鼓掌歡呼，有些同學還問我如何能做到吃得如此健康，這真是我最得意的一刻了！

　　老師又問：「很多食安問題是因食物過度加工所引起，班上誰最少吃過度精緻加工的食物？」班上同學再次將目光注視在我身上！

　　「如如這樣吃也是為了要兼顧六大營養成分。看過食物原來的面貌，才知食物真滋味！如如是上天選擇的天使，來讓我們知道食物的原味，讓我們知道如何吃才是愛惜自己的身體！」聽到老師的描述，才知道我根本不必擔心食安問題，因為我吃的食物很少加工，原味最好，原味才是正道！而且我還是飄逸善良的飲食天使呢！

老師最後告訴全班：「自己的身體自己顧，能堅持愛惜自己才是勇敢；會照顧自己，不讓父母擔心才是孝順！我們班上誰是最勇敢又孝順的孩子呢？」同學們在這節課第三次將眼光轉向我，我是大家公認有勇氣又孝順的孩子，哈哈哈！

　　世界上有些東西不一定要吃到或吃盡，留點餘念會更有滋有味！我很幸運，因為我從一開始就只能好好吃，不能隨便吃！

　　那天之後我明白了，我的飲食是一種健康快樂餐，大家都可以這麼吃！畢竟像老師說的：「為了五十年後還能快樂相見的同學會，我們要好好愛惜自己！」

　　台灣近年來接連爆發食安事件，不禁讓筆者聯想到以下幾點：(1)飲食西化造成兒童肥胖、營養不均與心血管疾病的案例日增；(2)社會陸續爆發竄改食品標示、食用期限，以及藥物殘留等食品安全事件；(3)鄰國日本曾因過度依賴進口糧食，導致自給率節節下降後，於 2005 年訂定《食育基本法》，並建立「營養教師」制度，特別在五育之外，又創造「食育」的概念，希望從兒童與青少年時期就建立正確的飲食知識與能力，以降低文明病的發生率，並推展維護傳統良好的飲食文化，強調確保食品的安全性及安心消費乃健全飲食生活的基礎。

　　糖尿病患者須盡可能在日常飲食上採取低 GI 食物。其實低「GI」（Glycemic index，升糖指數之簡稱）的飲食（參見附錄）基本上頗符合前述飲食教育的原則，但筆者在教育現場卻常看到許多患有第一型糖尿病需控制飲食的患童不是被教導如何正確吃低「GI」飲食，而是被教導盡可能少吃；然而任何食物都可能造成血糖上升，致使許多孩子在吃東西的過程中充滿罪惡感。再加上一起分享美食是台灣社交文化中重要的一環，也影響了孩子在校內的社交生活，總覺得自己跟同學在校內的相處像能看見彼此，卻因食物的關係而無法了解彼此。以上種種促使筆者決定寫這本繪本。筆者覺得台灣在前面所說的食安事件、飲食西化造成問題及日本《食育基本法》的訂定之後，也應該要推展飲食教育，教大家如何「好好吃」，並學會感謝與珍惜食物。購買食物前更要注意一些原則，例如：食品被加工到看不出食物原來型態的盡可能不要吃；食品添加物超過三項以上的盡可能不要吃；食品添加物中有看不懂的說明盡可能不要吃。進而讓食品商及餐飲業跟著消費者飲食教育後的習慣走，學會提供健康的食物給大家！

附 錄

常見食物 GI 指數表（升糖指數表）

　　「GI」（Glycemic index 的簡稱），中文稱為「升糖指數」，代表我們吃進的食物造成血糖上升速度快慢的數值。吃進較高 GI 值的食物，血糖上升速度便會較快，相反的，吃進較低 GI 值的食物，血糖上升速度則較慢；但因為食物的種類、烹調方式、來源及含纖維量的不同，GI 值也會產生不同。

　　一般來說，含糖量或碳水化合物較高的食物（例如：精緻糕點麵包、白飯、糯米飯等），GI值會較高，吃進這些食物會加速血糖上升，容易引起飢餓感而誘發食慾，無意間增加進食量，並容易大量產生脂肪，增加人體血液或細胞中脂肪的堆積，對於糖尿病人血糖控制或欲減重者體重控制尤為不利；對一般民眾來說，也會影響血糖的穩定性及提高代謝症候群、心血管疾病發生的風險。相反來說，纖維質較豐富的食物（例如：含纖維豐富的全穀類食物及蔬菜等），GI 值則較低，攝取這些食物，餐後血糖上升的速度會較為緩慢，對於血糖、血脂與體重的控制，及減少罹患代謝症候群、糖尿病、心臟病等慢性疾病風險都有很大幫助。

　　但我們難免會碰到或非常想吃某些高GI食物，建議這時可搭配GI較低的食物一起食用，例如：吃白飯或糯米飯時，多配些蔬菜一起吃；吃白吐司時夾生菜沙拉等，都能有效平衡食物的 GI 值。特別是已有糖尿病、心血管疾病、代謝症候群或體重過重的情形時，平常的主食宜盡量選擇低 GI 的食物（如五穀根莖類），較有利於疾病及體重的控制。只要多花一點心思了解各類食物特性，注意攝取的總量及烹調方式，同時注意均衡飲食，就能吃得更健康囉！

食物種類	食物 GI 指數（以白麵包 GI ＝ 100 作為 GI 食物對照之參考指標）
	備註： 一般來說是用「葡萄糖」當 100（低 GI 約 55～60 以下） 衛服部資料是用「白麵包」當 100（低 GI 約 75～80 以下） 以下表格資料，GI 值超過 80 者，標示為紅字，因為食物種類繁多，以下僅列舉兒童較常食用的食物為例。
五穀根莖類	全麥早餐穀類 GI ＝ 43 ± 3 粉絲 GI ＝ 56 ± 13 義大利麵 GI ＝ 60 ± 4 米粉 GI ＝ 61 ± 6 速食麵 GI ＝ 67 ± 2 綠豆 GI ＝ 76 ± 11 甜玉米 GI ＝ 78 ± 6 烏龍麵 GI ＝ 79 ± 10 燕麥片粥 GI ＝ 83 ± 5 烤馬鈴薯 GI ＝ 85 ± 4 甘藷 GI ＝ 87 ± 10 玉米脆片 GI ＝ 90 ± 15 白米飯 GI ＝ 91 ± 9 白麵包 GI ＝ 100 薯條 GI ＝ 107 ± 6 糯米飯 GI ＝ 132 ± 9
蔬菜類	菜豆 GI ＝ 39 ± 6 扁豆 GI ＝ 41 ± 1 大豌豆（夾）GI ＝ 56 ± 12 胡蘿蔔 GI ＝ 68 ± 23
豆類	黃豆 GI ＝ 25 ± 4
水果類	櫻桃 GI ＝ 32 葡萄柚 GI ＝ 36 蘋果 GI ＝ 52 ± 3 草莓 GI ＝ 57 蘋果汁 GI ＝ 57 ± 1 柳橙 GI ＝ 60 ± 5 柳橙汁 GI ＝ 71 ± 5 芒果 GI ＝ 73 ± 8 草莓果醬 GI ＝ 73 ± 14 香蕉 GI ＝ 74 ± 5 奇異果 GI ＝ 75 ± 8

水果類	小紅莓汁 GI = 80 木瓜 GI = 84 ± 2 鳳梨 GI = 84 ± 11 西瓜 GI = 103
乳製品類	全脂牛奶 GI = 38 ± 6 優格 GI = 51 布丁 GI = 62 ± 5 豆奶 GI = 63 冰淇淋 GI = 87 ± 10
烘培食品類	蛋糕（蛋糕粉）GI = 60 海棉蛋糕 GI = 66 鬆餅 GI = 78 ± 6 糖霜雞蛋糕 GI = 104 甜甜圈 GI = 108 ± 10
零食點心類	腰果 GI = 31 花生 GI = 47 巧克力 GI = 61 ± 4 洋芋片 GI = 77 ± 4 爆米花 GI = 103 ± 24
碳酸飲料類	可口可樂 GI = 83 ± 7 芬達汽水 GI = 97
糖類	果糖 GI = 27 ± 4 乳糖 GI = 66 ± 3 蜂蜜 GI = 78 ± 7 蔗糖 GI = 97 ± 7 葡萄糖 GI = 141 ± 4

資料來源：整理自：http://www.doh.gov.tw/CHT2006/DM/DM2_p01.aspx? class_no=25&level_no=1&doc_no=75802
Foster-Powell, K., Holt, S. H., & Brand-Miller, J. C. (2002). International table of glycemic index and glycemic load values. *Am J Clin Nutr, 76*(1), 5-56.
https://www.ncbi.nlm.nih.gov/pubmed/12081815

Eating Properly Is All I Can Do

Written by Ying-Ru Meng
Illustrated by Jia-Hao Wen & Wan-Ting Wen
Translated by Arik Wu

All I can do is to eat properly. Yes, eating properly is all I can do!

Ru Ru is my name. I was diagnosed with type 1 diabetes at a young age. Since then, I have learned to live with my high blood glucose level. "Always eat a fixed amount of food and stick to regular mealtimes. Eating foods in moderate amounts and doing exercise regularly are the keys to longevity," doctors always say to me.

Any food that is high in sugar, sodium, fat, or cholesterol is taboo to me.

Since most school lunches are taboo to me, all I can eat are only my multigrain rice, vegetables, and fish.

In school, lunch breaks are usually the time when my classmates throw birthday parties. With tables of soda, cokes, Yakult, jellies, puddings, and candy, everyone is having a blast, except for me. I can only sit there watching them and eating the guavas and tomatoes my mom has prepared for me.

Doing exercise on a regular basis is very important for me. However, I can never have a cup of bubble milk tea or any cold drinks after physical education classes. Even after school, I am still not allowed to feast on hot dogs, red bean wheel pies, ice creams, or Slurpees on my way home like other classmates do.

On Mondays or days after holidays, my classmates always gather together to talk about what they ate during the off-days. When they mention food names such as chicken cutlets, chicken nuggets, pork knuckles, and crispy butter cakes, I just feel like a square peg in a round hole... Sometimes, I really envy that they get to eat everything as much as they please.

Going out together to have delicacies or group buying are also their favorite activities. They rarely invite me, though. Even if they do, I always end up a bummer and ruin their appetite completely because most foods are taboo to me. What can I do? I do not know!

At times, some of my classmates like to tease me by eating fried chicken legs or foods that are detrimental to my health in front of me. "This smells so good! Ru Ru, you just don't know how to enjoy good foods," they say. "Life without these delicacies wouldn't be as enjoyable!"

"Don't seduce me!" I say jokingly. "For me, eating something improper is like skating on thin ice. My life will be in danger!"

A number of my classmates do not understand my condition, and assume that the reason why I eat a moderate, fixed amount of foods is because I want to stay slim. Thus, they always worry about my health and bring me snacks in secret for fear that I may be malnourished.

Somehow, I feel like today's class is going to be a turning point in my life.

The topic for today's discussion is "How to Eat Properly? Take A Look at Recent Food Scandals!"

"We cannot live without foods, but what can we do to keep our health? We should always eat properly, instead of swallowing whatever that comes in our way," Teacher says. Her words grab my attention immediately. This is exactly what doctors and diabetes educators have been telling me all the time!

Teacher then shows us an elaborate PowerPoint presentation that reads, "Recent food scandals: in 2011, more than fifty beverages and food products, such as fruit juice concentrate powders, fruit jams and syrups, juices, and yoghurt powders, were contaminated with plasticizers. In 2014, a variety of plastic-packaged food products were also contaminated with plasticizers."

Upon reading these words, many of my classmates gasp in disbelief, "My goodness! These are what I drink every once in a while!"

"Also, in 2013, many food products, such as Hakka flat noodles and tapioca balls, were found to be tainted with maleic anhydride," Teacher continues. Her words make the whole class even more terrified. "These are all my favorites!" they say.

"In 2013, a bakery was found to be adding artificial flavorings into its bread," Teacher says. "That bakery was really famous! My mom even waited in line for hours for its bread," one classmate says.

"Many leavening agents that were used to make bread at that time had aluminum. Bread and toast were all tainted!" Teacher resumes. "I always eat a loaf of bread for breakfast, sometimes even two! Yuck!" another classmate responds.

"Again, in 2013, many cooking oil products were discovered to be blended with cheaper cottonseed and sunflower oils and have contained sodium copper chlorophyllin, a coloring agent for cooking oil," Teacher says. "The influence of this food scandal has been really far-reaching."

"That's right! Back then, there were also two cans of tainted cooking oils at my home. My mom loved buying them at malls because they were often at a discount. Well, we dare not use any of those cooking oils anymore," yet another classmate says.

"Popiah skins were discovered to have contained Rongalit!" Teacher says. "Popiah is my favorite snack!" one classmate lets out a loud scream.

"A great number of tea beverages also contain pesticides," Teacher adds, which silences the whole class instantly, for some of them drink at least one cup every day.

"So, who has the healthiest diet in the class?" Teacher asks. Everyone quickly turns around to look at me, claiming unanimously, "Ru Ru has the healthiest diet in the class!"

"Ru Ru is most capable of resisting junk food!"

"Ru Ru always eats properly!"

"Ru Ru always eats a fixed amount of food and stick to regular mealtimes. She even does exercise regularly!"

"That's right! Ru Ru has the healthiest diet in our class! She doesn't need to panic about the food scandals because she always takes every meal seriously. As long as she eats the right foods at the right time and with just the right amount, she should lead a healthy life," Teacher says. "Let us give Ru Ru a big hand for having the healthiest diet in the class!"

I stand up to receive the applause, and some classmates come over to ask me how I am able to eat so properly. This has truly been the happiest moment in my life!

1. Staple foods
2. Dairy foods
3. Eggs
6. Vegetables & Fruits
5. Legume
4. Fish & Meat

"Most food scandals were caused by over-processing. So, who eats the least processed foods among us?" Teacher poses another question, which has everybody turn around to look at me again.

"Ru Ru is an angel! She teaches us how to enjoy the original flavors of foods and to tell us what we can do to keep our health!" Teacher continues. Now, not only do I understand that I have nothing to panic about because my diet seldom includes processed foods, but I also realize that I am a kind and graceful angel! Original flavors are the best!

"Only when we learn how to take good care of ourselves can we be seen as smart, and only when we learn not to worry our parents can we be deemed filial pious." Teacher says. "So, who is the smartest and most filial pious in our class?"

For the third time during this class period, everybody turns around to look at me. Oops! Am I also the smartest and most filial pious person in the class?

In life, we do not have to eat every delicacy or finish up everything that is served to us. Sometimes, this will make our lives even more colorful and meaningful!

How blessed I am to have learned the importance of eating proper early in my life. Now, I understand that my diet can be both healthy and enjoyable! Everyone can follow this diet! After all, we all want to be able to "reunite fifty years later without missing any one of us," as Teacher puts it. And that, requires us to take good care of ourselves.